# FROM CHASING DOPE
# TO PUSHING HOPE
## My Steps To Recovery & Redemption

Scott Hartman

# "I asked for strength

and God gave me difficulties to make me strong.

# I asked for wisdom

and God gave me problems to learn to solve.

# I asked for prosperity

and God gave me a brain and brawn to work.

# I asked for courage

and God gave me dangers to overcome.

# I asked for love

and God gave me people to help.

# I asked for favours

and God gave me opportunities.

*I received nothing I wanted.*
*I received everything I needed."*

— Hazrat Inayat Khan

# Forward

I interviewed Scott a few years ago over the phone for a recovery video series. His story really has made a difference! It's been a pleasure to meet him in person and see a life changed by God! This is a book for the addict, person in recovery, friends and family of those struggling with addiction and anyone who wants to truly understand the mind of someone in addiction and recovery.

**Shane Reinert**
Addictions Series Youube

# Contents

# Dedication

In writing this story of my life I've hurt a lot of people. I've lost relationships, watched people pass, and squndered moments. One relationship I have is like looking through a window at your life knowing I'm not a part of it, but so proud of the Man you have become, Tyler, my son.

# Prelude

2 Corithians 5:8

*We live by Faith not by sight..*

The Cincinnati/Northern Kentucky International Airport (CVG) is an unusual place to be starting to tell my story. This journey I'm on began a week ago in St. Charles, MO – a river town just west of St. Louis, Missouri, where I currently call home. Here at the CVG Airport, I'm considering the remainder of my trip, which will take me to Crossville, Tennessee, back to Cincinnati, Ohio, and on to Dallas, Texas, before I return home. Beyond this, I'm unsure of my next move; but as I sit here, I recognize that I'm truly blessed to be where I'm today. I'm meeting amazing people all along the way as I speak about God, recovery, and life...a journey I never thought I would live to take. Though I'm sitting here at the airport alone, this is not a solo trip; it is also an invitation to you the reader in joining me on a journey that will hopefully change your life as it has changed mine.

**But wait – I need to start at the beginning.**

# Chapter One: Das Scott Hartman

## Jeremiah 29:11

*For i know the plans i have for you, declares the Lord, plans to prosper you and not harm you, plans to give you hope and a future..*

I was born Scott Arthur Hartman on December 2, 1970; the son of Robert and Polly Hartman. My dad was early in his career in the U.S. Army, from which he retired several years later. Though I was very young at the time, my memory of living in Germany still remains, and I have amazing memories of our life in Munich, Heidelberg, and Frankfurt, I still recall the Alpine beauty; the snow-covered peaks, the green pastures, picturesque villages in the mountain valleys, and the storybook castles. Especially, I remember hikes in the forest with my parents and older sister. It was a time of innocence and wonder, but clouded by memories of family abuse.

I can't say that anything besides my father's addiction to alcohol and a violent temper was to blame for the abuse he inflicted on my mother and us. Perhaps the easy access to alcohol at the base clubs, culture of drinking, or the pressure of military life, in general, contributed to his descent into alcoholism. I recall that often, after being in the field on military exercises at Grafenwoehr or elsewhere, my father would return home drunk, and would take out his uncontrolled rage on my mother, sister, and me. This went on for a long time, and became so unbearable that Mom eventually packed us up and we left Germany... without Dad. They divorced shortly after that.

Our return to the States took us to the small town of Bonne Terre, Missouri, in Eastern Missouri. Founded by the French in the early 1700s, Bonne Terre (literally, the Good Earth) had been a thriving iron ore mining town for over a hundred years. But by the 1970's, the mines had closed, and what remained was a sleepy, obscure little community. We traded the deep valleys and Alpine beauty of Southern Germany for the mine-scarred soil of rural Missouri. But we were safe. It was there we lived with my grandmother and uncle for a while, before moving several more times and finally settling near St. Louis in Festus, Missouri. Festus was a little larger community, and as I approached my teenage years, I faced the challenge of adjusting to yet another move, new school, and new friends.

The many moves with the military, the divorce, and frequent changes of address and schools as a young boy, had made it difficult for me to make friends, especially long-term friends. So, by the time I was in middle school in Festus, I felt like an outcast; I wasn't very out-going, and didn't know how to fit in or where I belonged. Seeking acceptance and recognition, I began to look for attention in any way I could from my family and my peers. This would lead to a dangerous pattern of behavior that, at the time, I couldn't have predicted. I was young and insecure, and craved stability and acceptance.

My mom was my hero; absolutely the strongest woman I knew. She worked two jobs, went to school, and tried to make life better for my older sister, Laura, and me. I loved my sister and wanted to have a good relationship with her, but we never became close, and I still don't understand why. Perhaps even at that early age, our lives were destined to take different paths.

While I was in middle school, Mom took a job at the local hospital. It was there that she met her second husband, a man with two sons and a daughter. I was 12 or 13 when they married. At first, the blended family idea was novel and fun, and it seemed to be working. We all got along, but looking back, though, I think it was probably because it was all new and everyone was on their best behavior. For the next few years, our family experienced some good moments, but which obscured the secret that would take years for me to share, much less face.

I cannot recall exactly when or how it began that my stepfather began to sexually abuse me, but it became the secret that was never to be shared for many years. As a teenage boy, my own hormones were raging, and I struggled with the conflict of thinking that I had some- how invited the abuse that went on, unnoticed, in our home. Was it a false sense of love and acceptance that I craved? Was I the only one being abused? What about his own children, or my sister? Did he abuse them, too? Did I deserve the pain of being sodomized repeatedly by this man who I had grown to trust as a stepfather? Did my mother, or anyone else in the family, notice this was going on? Was it the "elephant in the room" that nobody would talk about?

The pain, the shame, the anger, the nightmare of having

this horrible secret that I couldn't – dare not – share, tormented me day after day. The fear of not being believed, or worse – of being ridiculed – forced me to keep silent, and led me to self-destructive and wrong behavior that would have terrible results.

Those of us who have experienced being sexually abused often feel that we are totally alone in our experiences; that we can't share them with anyone without fear of retaliation or exposure. We may feel ambivalent – having mixed feelings or conflicting ideas about what's happened – which leads to more shame and anger. But we are not alone: According to studies, more than 14% of boys under the age of 18 are sexually abused. This figure may be low, however, since many boys, like myself, are reluctant or afraid to report it. Further, boys represent half of all of the children who are sexually trafficked. Today, we are becoming more aware and willing to speak out about the horrible crimes against children, and there are people who will listen and respond. But as a confused teen in the 1980s, this was the humiliating shame that no young man would admit.

*Some reading this may understand, if you've had your own experience of being sexually, physically, emotionally, and/ or psychologically abused as a child or adult. You understand how it leaves scars on our minds and spirits – scars*

*too deep, too intimate and personal, to be shared without*
*pain and fear. If you are one of those young people or adult*
*victims of abuse, know that there is no condemnation, no*
*guilt, no blame. Seek help and safe support. There is a way*
*out, and there is healing. I experienced it, and you can, too.*
*I'll share with you how I found it.*

During those teenage years in school, I tried to cover my
hurt and confusion by becoming involved in sports and
band. Rather than feeling a greater sense of identity and
acceptance, I became more and more inside myself. I
tried to put up a good front, however, and even though
I was shy, people would reach out to me for relationship
advice. I didn't see the irony of that at the time – I didn't
recognize what a healthy relationship was - I only knew
I wanted to be accepted and liked for who I was. So,
school friends would call and I would tie up the house
phone every evening, driving my mother and sister crazy (note to younger readers: These were pre-cell phone
days!).

Being sought out for advice built my confidence some-
what and my feeling of acceptance, but it didn't ease
the loneliness, hurt, and shame that I felt. What if they
knew what I held inside? To deal with it, I lashed out by
constantly getting into fights, both in and out of school,
and causing chaos in the neighborhood. I was so angry

one night with some neighbors and their kids, I convinced some friends to gather all the "House for Sale" signs we could steal from neighborhood yards and put them in front of one particular house. There must have been 100 signs in that yard! I was the kid who would take one bulb out of a string of Christmas lights on a house just to see them all go out. I'd stand back and laugh as the home-owner tried to figure out the problem. One night, friends and I took part of a dunking booth set up for a carnival, and pushed it down a long hill and through a neighbor's fence. As an increasingly reckless teen, I didn't think of the inconvenience and damage any of these acts of van-dalism caused; to me it was a funny and harmless way of acting out and retaliating against people who made me mad. And it got me noticed. We were caught in that last act, however, and disciplined over the fence incident. As part of our punishment were made to return the dunking booth where we found it, which involved pushing the bulky frame back up the hill!

I still didn't get it, though, or imagine where this rebellion and destructiveness would take me. Eventually, my be-havior took me in a dangerous direction that would take me years to escape…

# Chapter Two: Hey Doc.

### Romans 5;8

*While we were sinners, Christ died for us...*

The trauma I experienced as a youth had set the stage for my downward spiral. Today, I look back with awful regret at my actions, and how my actions impacted others. As a recovering addict, I can now reflect on some of my past behaviors and see signs of addictive behavior before substance abuse took over my life. Among other things, I began to show signs of obsessive-compulsive disorder (OCD). This involves troubling thoughts, impulses, or images that are repeated over and over. They can be strong, frightening, silly, or unusual, and result in actions and behavior that become bizarre and irrational rituals. For example, I watched the same TV shows over and over, ate the same food items for days on end, and listened to the same songs for hours at a time. If I liked something, I took it to excessive levels. People began to notice and comment on my behavior, and not favorably.

At age 16, I felt that I was finally achieving the recognition and acceptance that I craved. It was 1986, and I got my first job at the Spinning Wheels Roller Skating Rink in Crystal City. I had arrived! My skill as an excellent skater and wearing the uniform of a skate guard seemed to draw people to me, and made me feel important. For the first time, I began to feel accepted by others. I made a lot of friends, dated a lot of girls, and was told that other girls had crushes on me. It was heady stuff, and I thrived on the attention and popularity that I was gaining.

In addition to working as a skate guard at Spinning Wheels, I also had a part-time job as a cart pusher at the local Shop 'N Save Grocery Store. My newly-acquired income and growing popularity gave me more easy access to alcohol, and it was during that time that I began to drink. And drink more and more. And more.

Then it happened.

Shortly before Thanksgiving, I was asked to retrieve Thanksgiving decorations from the top of a cooler. As I climbed on top of the cooler, I lost my balance, and fell 12 feet through a drop ceiling, and landed on a steel meat wrapping table. The ambulance arrived and took me to the hospital, where I had x-rays, and assured that nothing was broken. I walked out of the Emergency Room following that incident.

The next day, however, I began to experience horrible pain which put me flat on my back for three weeks. The doctor's prescription for pain medication was extremely generous, and I took full advantage of it. He could have had no idea how dangerous that would be for me, though. I discovered a new high – a new thrill, a new buzz – that I had not experienced before. The pills made me feel amazing – invincible, outgoing, whole – and accepted. Under the constant influence of prescription medications, I could forget – for a little while, at least - the abuse and trauma of my childhood. Later I realized that drugs medicate pain – not just the physical pain of my, but emotional and psychological, as well.

Since I was still under the doctor's care, I wasn't released to return to work at the roller rink; however, I went to the rink on weekends to hang out with friends, and as I said, met and dated many girls. One of those girls was the most beautiful young lady I would ever know. Her name was Abby.[1] We weren't into our relationship very long before my mother threw me out of the house for kicking the dog, after it chewed up my underwear. I realized later that my behavior was becoming destructive not only to myself, but I was taking out my uncontrollable anger on others, including my dog. At the time I couldn't see that, though – I was beginning to exhibit a growing anger and patterns of addictive thinking that wouldn't allow me to see how my behavior was hurting everything and every-one who I cared about.

I moved in with my new girlfriend, the love of my life, and I was certain we would spend the remainder of our lives together. I had found someone who would care for me despite my erratic and explosive behavior. Things were looking up, and life was good for a time. However, the mental demons returned to torment me as I got deeper and deeper into my addiction, and my behavior began to affect our relationship. The girl loved me, but I didn't – couldn't – love myself. In my mind, I still had no self-worth.

I was still receiving Worker's Compensation from the fall, and had made arrangements to have the checks sent to my new address at my girlfriend's house. At first, I didn't

---

1        Not her real name

know that the checks were continuing to go to my parents' address, though. It wasn't until I tried to buy my first car that I realized I had a black mark on my credit, and discovered that my stepfather – the same man who sodomized me – had stolen my checks, forged my name, and cashed them to feed his own addiction to pain medications.

When I told my mother, she shrugged it off. She said he had a problem, he's sorry, and what more could she do? The violation I had experienced at his hands years before was reawakened and intensified by the betrayal I felt from my mother, who enabled his addiction and criminal behavior. Of course, he never apologized for stealing my checks and forging my identity, and if he was sorry, he never admitted it, at least to me. My mother's dismissal of the whole issue felt like a kick in my gut, because I had counted on her to be supportive. My disappointment and anger were rekindled, which led to me drinking more, and starting to smoke pot, as well as taking pain medication. That's the only way I knew to cope with my feelings of betrayal. The saying "drugs medicate pain" was becoming all too real for me.

In the midst of all this, Abby and I became engaged. I knew I wanted to be a good husband to her, but I continued to be haunted by the trauma and rejection of my past. The drugs were only a temporary fix, at best, to numb my feelings and alter my behavior, which was becoming worse. After this incident with my mother and stepfather, I began lashing out harder with fighting, and generally, becoming a neighborhood terror.

Living with Abby and her parents had its moments, but it wasn't long before we began arguing. In retrospect, I was causing a good part of the discord, and when the tension continued to escalate, I moved back to my mother's and stepfather's house for a brief time. As you can imagine, this was a terrible idea. Still struggling with the conflict and unresolved anger, I cut my wrists in desperation, resulting in my spending over a month in a psychiatric ward. I received counseling, and when I left, I thought I had things under control. This lasted for just a brief time. I continued to feel intense emotional pain and continued to see the doctor... who also fueled my prescription drug usage.

Against all odds, my girlfriend and I came back together, and in 1990 Abby and I were married. In the midst of the festivities, the day was marred by my grandmother making unkind remarks about my new bride in front of her. Once again, I felt the disapproval and rejection rise up. It was becoming a pattern in my life.

On the surface, my new wife, Abby, and I had a good life. We bought a new single-wide mobile home, and had a baby on the way. I was a husband and a father with a new car and a home. I should have been ecstatic, but the turmoil in my mind continued. I was a train wreck waiting to happen. I tried to bury my torment in work. I was employed at a grocery store, working midnights to 6:30 am, determined to be a responsible husband and father. However, within 15 minutes of leaving work, I had a beer in my hand to begin the hour-long drive home. The six-pack would be gone when I arrived home.

Two years into our marriage, a neighbor introduced Abby and me to the Amway home business. I was excited to try it, but my wife wasn't interested. I was – and remain – a dreamer and a follower, and was hoping that a home-based business would allow me to become more accepted, solve my problems, and be happy. I couldn't begin to define what acceptance, problem solution and happiness looked like – or if I'd recognize them if I found them – but I was certain that this would be my ticket to success and "happiness".

I didn't get it.

So, I eagerly went to my first Amway convention in Springfield, MO, only to come home two days later to an empty house.  My wife had taken our small son and moved out.  All those long hours of work hadn't made a difference, I thought.  It should come as no surprise, at this point, that I was still unable or unwilling then to admit to the destructive behaviors that had destroyed my marriage – and continued to destroy my life.

I was devastated, sure that my world was coming to an end.  Why would she just leave like that?  Where to turn?  God?  I was raised in church and taught that I should trust God.  But my growing years, dysfunctional home life, and unfolding life experiences didn't give me much – if any – of a foundation or idea of what trusting God would look like. And if I had no idea of what that trust would look like, I also couldn't imagine what trusting Him could possibly involve.  Sunday School teachings about the goodness of the Lord and putting our trust in Him didn't seem to register in my broken heart and fogged-up brain.  If I prayed for help, He'd answer right away in just the way I expected, right?

Nope, I still didn't get it. It took me two more decades of destructive living with addiction and broken lives to understand about surrendering everything to Him.  But that day, facing the reality of losing my wife and child, God wasn't in the picture.

For the next several months, I immersed myself in work, and during weekend visitation, spent time with my little son; otherwise, I isolated myself, and tried to save my marriage. I feared that I would lose the mobile home, car, and everything else in the divorce. I felt hopeless. Then one night, I went to a free concert sponsored by a local rock station, and something inside of me broke loose.

It was a next step in the downward spiral of my addiction and self-destructive behavior.

About that time, I began a new job working at a restaurant during the day and continuing my night job at the Shop 'N Save, and soon ran into an old buddy who introduced me to crystal meth.[2] He moved into the mobile home to help with bills, and beyond that, the next several months were a blur of drugs, parties, sex, chaos, and not much else. I went without sleep for days on end, putting drugs and alcohol above everything. The one exception was the time I was allowed to spend with my son, when I devoted myself to him. I thought I was making him a priority above even the drugs, but I was deceiving myself. I had no idea how my addiction and destructive behavior might have been affecting my relationship with him.

---

2        Short for crystal methamphetamine, also called "ice"; a white crystalline drug that people "snort", smoke, or inject with a needle. It is a strong and highly addictive drug that affects the central nervous system. It creates a quick rush of euphoria, but is dangerous, and can damage the body and cause severe psychological problems.

It was in the midst of this chaos that my natural father contacted me, saying he needed a place to stay. As you recall, he was an abusive alcoholic from my childhood, leading my mother to divorce him and move us back to Missouri. We had very little contact over the years since leaving Germany, but somehow, I thought all of that would be behind us. I remembered the hikes as a young boy in the Bavarian forests with my father, and though that maybe – just maybe – we could have a father-son relationship that we hadn't had in nearly two decades. It was food for hope. I had the room and needed the additional income, so I invited him to move in, with one stipulation: No drinking.

Now, if you're following the story, you'll see the irony of all that. Telling my alcoholic father not to have alcohol in my house was the height of hypocrisy, if nothing else. The stupidity of that escaped me at the time, as I was fully saturated in my own addictive behavior. I was busy having keg parties when I wasn't working, or trying to spend time with my son. But my father agreed to remain sober – perhaps just to pacify me, or may even hope to reconcile in some way. Keep in mind, not only did the beer flow and the drugs appear, but women were constantly coming in and out. My dad was seeing all of this, and sat in his room because he was told he couldn't drink.

So, it's no surprise, that pretty soon I began finding the whiskey bottles; hidden at first, then left around where they might be found. I confronted my dad and told him he would have to leave. The situation spiraled out of control quickly. Typical of my addictive thinking, I had expected him to do what I was unable/unwilling to do myself. The relationship rapidly became strained, and I remembered his drinking, the physical abuse, and the separation from him when I was a child. I was the child – the victim - all over again; he was the victimizer. I wasn't willing to admit how I had become an abusive addict myself. The generational pattern of addiction and abuse was being played out in my life, as well.

It wasn't until I was in recovery years later that I realized how very wrong I was. My father bore the brunt of the negative emotions I tried to keep buried; abandonment issues, the many moves, always trying to make friends, and the divorce. One day, it all came to a head in one horrendous fight between us that I have so often wished had never happened. My dad reached out to try to make the relationship right, but I wasn't ready. I thought I'd have time later to reconsider, and that when I was ready, we would talk on my terms, not his. I felt betrayed by another family member again, and to dull the pain, my drinking and drug use intensified as I was trying to hide things from my family.

Unfortunately, the time to talk and reconcile never came. A week later, my dad went to sleep and didn't wake up.

He was just 54 when he died; a lonely man, defeated by his own addictions and failures. Multiple marriages, years of alcohol abuse, and life crises had left him a broken man. My dad fought his own personal demons, as well, but I couldn't see it; I was blinded by my own anger, resentment, and regret. In the end, he tried to make our relationship right, but it didn't happen. It was at that moment I was confronted – perhaps for the first time – with the damage that my own addictive behavior could create; however, I still wasn't ready to accept it.

My dad was buried at the Jefferson Barracks National Cemetery in St. Louis; a beautiful and serene cemetery on the bluffs above the banks of the Mississippi River, which is the final resting place for nearly 200,000 soldiers and spouses. In a shaded grove are the weathered gravestones of Civil War soldiers, and rolling acres of markers for those who served in the World Wars, Korea, Viet Nam, the Iraqi War, as well as those who served in peacetime. My father died in the war with alcohol, and found peace at last in this place.

It took me 20 years to get past my own pain and self-centered focus to visit my father's grave. It was like putting someone like me in a dope house with drugs in front of me, and saying "Look, but don't touch." I could never bring back that opportunity to heal a relationship that had cost me so much of my childhood and youth. My father had tried in the only way he knew, and I rejected him in the end. The chance to find healing and closure in my relationship with my father never happened.

# Chapter Three: Fall Into It

## 1 Peter 1;3-5

*We have an incredible hope. But sometimes life can "get in the way' and it can be hard to hold on to that hope..*

The death of my father could have been my wake-up call to recognize the seriousness of my addiction, but it wasn't.

All the damaging events in my life and my negative emotions swirled in my mind, as I continued to numb it with hard partying. It was the '90s, and crystal meth, cocaine, and pot, along with Jack and Coke®,[3] were my "vitamins" to get me through life. Work, drugs, and sex

---

3    Jack Daniels® Whiskey and Coca-Cola®

consumed my life, as I continued to damage others' lives as well as my own, continuing to careen along my own destructive path.

As often happened, I would stay awake for days at a time when I was partying and drugging... and since that was almost constantly, you can imagine that my body and mind were dangerously suffering from sleep deprivation and the effects of the drugs. On July 4, 1992, I could no longer go without sleep; my body finally crashed, and I overslept for work. My employer had been cutting me some slack because of the divorce and other things I was going through, but this time I had pushed it too far. I knew if I didn't show up for work that I would lose a good-paying job. I freaked out, rolled a joint, and in that moment, knew that something had to change. I packed some clothes and checked myself into the hospital in Festus, MO, for treatment.

I thought I was starting to get it.

The doctors told me that another two weeks or so of staying on the damaging path I was on would have killed me. That path was rapidly leading to self-destruction and was nearly completed. I had come to the place where I didn't care. Yet. in some more coherent recess in my mind, I realized I still had some will to live. So I entered treatment and stuck it out.

I had also come to the right place to save my life, and I'll forever be grateful to the staff and other participants who thought I was worth saving and restoring. I spent 32 days in residential treatment. It was my first journey into drug treatment; 32 days to get clean, rest my body, eat a proper diet, and begin a process of treatment and reha- bilitation. By the time I was ready to leave, I was allowed to run some group meetings while the techs[4] were pres- ent, and I was offered a job on the floor provided I took ten credit hours of classes to earn my certification.

When I left treatment, I thought I was strong enough to stay clean and go to school. For those of you who have been there and get it, you're probably nodding your heads in understanding. You can guess that I wasn't ready for what was ahead, and was headed for a fall. But for a brief, exhilarating time, I felt empowered that I could take what I learned in four weeks and successfully solo the rest of my recovery. Residential treatment had mer- cifully removed me from imminent death-by-drugs, but didn't prepare me to face the challenges once I hit the streets again. I was cleaned up and cleaned out, and my head was clearer for the first time in a long, long time. I had gained some valuable tools, but lacked the blueprint

---

4        Treatment technicians

for taking those tools to begin to rebuild and reshape my life after addiction. Recovery, I would learn, is a journey – it's not a one-time thing or an "aha moment". I wasn't ready to go it alone – I would never be. You know that, right? But I didn't know that.

I didn't get that detail yet.

Fresh out of recovery, I tried attending two recovery meetings, but decided they weren't for me. I could do this on my own with the tools I'd been given. After all, I was entrusted to lead some groups in treatment and offered an opportunity to work with them, so I must be "cured". That was the first red flag. Being brand-new to recovery, I didn't realize that, without support and a strong recovery plan, my addiction – and my addictive thinking and behavior – would draw me back into using sooner or later. It came sooner rather than later.

Instead of experiencing support and acceptance from my family, I felt more alone and separated from them than ever before. No one in my family knew the depth of my addiction and the personal pain that fueled it. I knew that something was missing in my life, that "something" had left a huge void long ago. I couldn't figure out how to "fix me" on my own. Support meetings weren't working for me, and I had tried religion, going in and out of churches. Each time I found a new church, I was sure it was going to be a new start, with new friendships, a new home, a new walk with God. But whenever I asked God for something and it didn't happen in my time or the way I thought it would/should happen, I was more convinced that He was either punishing me, had forgotten about me, or worse – He hated me. I thought I had destroyed my life so badly that there was no hope from treatment, from family, from recovery meetings… or from God.

In the following chapters, you'll learn just how wrong I was.

Meanwhile, it took me practically no time at all to fall back into the depths of my addiction. Having decided that I didn't need meetings and recovery support, I was again going to doctors for pain pills, using meth, and drinking nonstop, while trying to keep it a secret from everyone. Self-deception is one of the hallmarks of the addictive personality and mind. We usually fool nobody but ourselves. Soon, my life was spinning out of control again. My best intentions to stay clean and sober evaporated in the familiar winds of manipulating, lying, cheating, hurting others to get what I wanted – sex, drugs, money, attention, appreciation, feeling wanted, or whatever.

*A basic difference between healthy people and addicted*

*people can be summarized in this: Healthy people use*
*"things" and have relationships with people. Addicts have*
*it backwards: We use people, and have relationships with*
*"things" – whether it's drugs, money, sex, gambling, or other*
*addictive habits and behaviors.*

Fast forward through five or six years of this kind of reckless, destructive behavior, and it is 1996. I was on my
way to a party with two gorgeous women when we were
pulled over by the police. I figured it was only a matter
of time before this would happen. I was arrested and
charged with possession of more than 35 grams of marijuana, with intent to distribute, and given a $20,000 bond
and five years' probation. This was reduced because I
completed my community service without causing any
trouble. However, it didn't slow down my partying. I
went at it even harder.

I was also willing to help anyone, regardless of the outcome. My ongoing craving for drugs was matched by
my craving for approval and acceptance by others, which
occasionally put me in compromising situations. I hoped
that by helping others, they would approve of me and
I would feel better about myself. The world continued
to revolve around me and my ungratified needs. Surely
there had to be more to life than this? I considered that
from time to time, and would cry out to God, thinking

perhaps – this time – He would remarkably or magically get me out of the pit I was digging deeper and deeper for myself.

God was, indeed, at work in me all during those days, in imperceptible ways that I didn't understand. I was still expecting God – like my earthly father – to meet me on my terms. I sometimes remembered two of my favorite stories from the Bible that I thought somehow applied to my life, and I could recall them in the quiet times when I found myself alone with my own thoughts and prayers: The story of David and Goliath,[5] and the story of Shadrach, Meshach, and Abednego.[6]

Nearly everyone knows the story of David and Goliath. It's a lesson of courage, faith, and overcoming something that seemed impossible. I wanted that. To recap the story, David was the youngest of Jessi's twelve sons. One day, the nation of Israel was called to fight the Philistine army that had gathered for war. David stayed at home while his brothers went to fight. A giant named Goliath, who stood over nine feet tall, came to the front of the Philistine battle line each day for forty days and mocked the Israelites and their God. While Goliath was taunting them and picking a fight, King Saul and the Israelite army were scared of him and his army, and did nothing. One day,

5        1 Samuel 17:
6        Daniel 3:

David's father sent him to the front lines to bring back news from his brothers, and he saw that the army was frightened. David was angered at Goliath's mocking God, and persuaded King Saul to let him go fight the giant. He refused to wear the king's armor against the huge bully, but simply carry his sling and five smooth stones to take him down.

You probably remember what happened then. Goliath threatened David with his huge sword and spear, but David came in the name of the Lord Almighty, the God of Israel, and slung a rock into the giant's forehead. Goliath came crashing to the ground, and David used the giant's sword to kill him and cut off his head. The Philistines fled. Game over. David was the hero that won the battle because, against all odds and doubts of those who were bigger and well-armed, he was willing to face the giant in his life because he knew that God was with him.

I wanted to be a giant-slayer, too.

Shadrach, Meshach, and Abednego were the three Hebrew men who were thrown into a fiery furnace by Nebuchadnezzar II, the King of Babylon, when they refused to bow down to worship the image of the king. The fire was hot enough to kill those who had stoked it, but then something amazing – miraculous - happened: Not only were the three men not killed, but when the king looked into the furnace, he saw a fourth person walking in the flames, "the fourth...like a son of God." Shadrack, Meshach, and Abednego emerged from the furnace un-burned – and they didn't even smell like smoke.

What was it about these three that caused such a miracle to occur? And if someone – like the son of God – could rescue them from the flames, could he do that for some-one like me? I didn't know if or how then, but the truths of those stories stuck with me during those days of rebel-lion and pain.

Meanwhile, emotionally and psychologically, I was still the scared little boy hiding his shame, and continued to feel alone, even in a crowd. I craved relationships and avoided spending time by myself. It may not have seemed obvious to others, but I was shy, and would cling to anyone who showed me attention or affection, and was heartbroken if my affections were not returned. I was the poster child for addictive co-dependency. My one coping skill was drugs and alcohol – the eternally tem-porary fix. Staying messed up all the time prevented me from facing my emotions, and reliving the traumas that has caused my emotional distress. The continual party-ing was destroying me and any relationship that I became a part of.

After my arrest, I lost my good-paying job at Shop 'N Save, and worse, my relationship with my son was deteriorating. I focused on finding employment, and answered an ad for selling vacuum cleaners door-to-door. I made some decent money at times, and managed to win a few trips, but I was still partying and in self-destruct mode. My meth use increased significantly, and my race to the bottom was accelerating faster and faster.

So, it should come as no surprise that I thought I'd hit the jackpot when I heard about sex shops that had video arcades in them. I hit every one of them within a fifty-mile radius, and wasn't finished discovering just how far I could descend. In these arcades, I watched porn on a TV screen, and allowed myself to engage in activities with others that I realized almost immediately were insane. I was high, alone, and feeling beat down. Any shred of self-esteem I may have had was lost in my need for gratification and relationship.

Even a bad relationship seemed better than none; That is, until one night, in my stupor, I ventured beyond bounds that even I would have considered dangerous and sick. I had agreed to pleasure another "patron" of the video arcade, but almost immediately stopped myself in shock. A wave of nausea washed over me like hot coals, and I was instantly alert and aware of how far I was allowing myself to fall. I literally ran from the video arcade and never looked back.

The impact of what I was doing hit me as I drove away. I swallowed hard, resisting the urge to throw up, as tears streamed down my face. What was wrong with me? What have I become? I wanted a loving relationship with a woman so badly, and couldn't ever manage how I would ever be able to make it happen. Was I really willing to settle for debasing and selling myself in a sex shop for a little dope or some phony affection? Why couldn't I be happy like other people?

These questions and more came rapid-fire through my mind as I sped away, choking down tears. At the time, I didn't realize that what I wanted was a "normal" life; but my life had been so far removed from what I pictured "normal" to be, that I didn't know what it would look like, or how to pursue or find it. Would I recognize "normal" if I ever found it? I didn't realize then that the life I had been living was my "normal". What other "normal" did I want?

I didn't realize then that there's a difference between what is normal and what is healthy. Those of us in recovery know that a major focus on recovery is developing healthy habits, healthy thoughts, healthy relationships, healthy activities, healthy bodies... healthy lives. We know when our lives are restored. Those things are not "normal" in an addictive lifestyle, and often, unfortunately, they are "normal" in the images we may create in our minds of how life will look in the absence of addiction and abuse.

After years of addiction, partying, orgies, homelessness, unemployment, and/or paying the dope man, entering into an idealized life of "normalcy" may take a while. At first, we may have to "couch surf" at the homes of others, may ride a bike or walk until we get a car, work at minimum wage while our bodies heal and we learn new skills to get better jobs. But we gain minds and bodies that are free from the oppression and tyranny of drugs and dangerous living, new relationships with other safe and healthy people, a release from the Goliaths in our lives that taunt and terrorize, telling us there is there is no hope, no victory, no way out... there is no God.

In that moment, all I felt was the revulsion of having hit a very low place in my life. I longed to fill the void in my heart that I'd had since childhood. Everything I was pursuing to hide the same, cover the insecurity, and fill the need for love and acceptance, didn't satisfy. Quite the opposite. My pursuit after love and fulfillment led me deeper and deeper still into despair and a lifestyle that was robbing me of meaning and life itself. Somewhere, somehow, I needed to find that piece of sanity, a place of rest for my soul.

It has been said that when the only tool you have is a hammer, you will view every problem as a nail. And to these "nails", I applied the only tools I knew: satisfy the craving in any way possible. So, when I heard some guys talking one night about where I could find cocaine and hookers, my eyes lit up like Christmas morning... here was something new I hadn't tried.

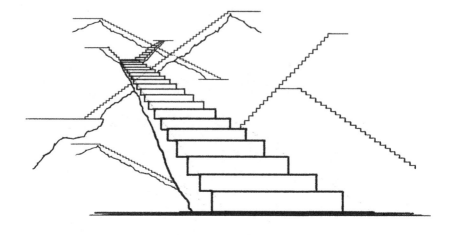

# Chapter Four: Revolving Door

**Psalm 4;8**

*In peace i will both lie down and sleep: for you alone,*
*O Lord, make me dwell in safety...*

In the midst of the confusion and drugs, I met Lisa[7],
who would become my second wife. She was 10 years
younger than me, had never been with another man, and
the fact that I was her first sent my frail, drug-soaked
ego through the roof. I tried to be a good husband, but
my unresolved issues made me damaged goods, and I
wasn't the supportive, attentive husband she needed.
When other women showed me attention, I was all over
it, which was so wrong.

---

7      Not her real name

Like me, Lisa had been sexually abused, which affected our intimacy, and though I was her first love, I felt cheated that I was somehow getting "damaged goods". A healthy person would not respond with such callous self-centeredness, but I wasn't healthy; by this point, it's evident that I was pretty well messed-up. I should have handled things differently, but characteristic of an addict, I was blind and deaf to the needs of others. What mattered to me was what my personal needs and self-esteem required. I had expected drugs and others to make me satisfied, and fulfill the real cravings I had for genuine loving relationships and acceptance.

Of course, it doesn't work that way. I continued to grow further and further apart from the people who meant the most to me in my life, including my young wife, my mother, and my sister. I avoided family gatherings or showed up late, and tried to be "sick" at holidays and birthdays. It was pathetic on my part, but I always did manage to show up, pretending illness, if there was good food and presents for me. I was still the black sheep of the family; still trying to hide what I had become.

You won't be surprised to learn that Lisa didn't remain in the marriage for very long. Who could blame her? To her credit, she salvaged what she could of her life with me, and moved on to find the love and intimacy that I couldn't

give her. Remember, addicts relate to things and use people, not the other way around. I didn't see it that way, of
course; I chalked up her leaving up as another failure in
my life to get my needs met, and it wasn't until years later
than I grasped and accepted the enormity of my wrongs.

Wife number three (yes, three) came along shortly after
Lisa left. She and I had dated in high school, and re-
connected on Face Book. We began dating again, and
characteristically, I was trying to hide my issues and addictions from her and those around us. I was so excited
that someone wanted to be with a person like me that I
allowed her to control the direction of the relationship. It
didn't matter if I was happy or not; what mattered to me
is that I wasn't alone. Co-dependency is one of the hallmarks of addictive relationships.

To be honest, I didn't want to go through with the marriage, but didn't have the guts to cancel it, and besides,
it might just be the satisfying relationship I was looking
for. So, to ease the reluctance and nervousness I felt, I
did the only thing I knew to do: I swallowed a handful
of muscle relaxers the day of the wedding to calm my
nerves.

*Remember, when the only tool you think you have is a ham-
mer, you will see every problem as a nail. I was still using*

*the only tool I thought I had.*

As a result of ingesting that many muscle relaxers, I wound up in the ER before the wedding. I remember being taken to the hospital by ambulance, but I don't remember much after that. My soon-to-be bride, her mother, and my mom convinced the doctor to release me to go to the wedding, which I also don't remember much about; only that it happened. I do remember that my best man kept his hands on my back to make sure I didn't fall over during the ceremony. By the time we got to my new in-law's house to celebrate, I was slowly coming around, but I was still far from being sober. As we opened gifts, I saw $300 in cash, and immediately my mind began to calculate how I could take it and go get high. Then on my wedding night, I found the opportunity.

My new wife woke me up with questions about text messages she found on my phone. In my wedding day drug-induced fog, some female friends texted me to see if I wanted to hang out, and I said yes. Seriously – I accepted invitations from other women on my wedding day. I'm not proud to admit that. I hadn't invited them to the wedding, or even say, no, sorry, I'm getting married today to a beautiful woman, maybe we could meet for drinks sometime? No. Instead, my new bride and I fought... and I held onto the $300.

You would be right on the money if you figure that this new marriage was about to go south pretty quick, and you, of course, would be right. In fact, marriage #3 only lasted four days. For me, the four days were a blur; for my new bride, they must've seemed like an eternity. On the fourth day, we went to a St. Louis Cardinal's baseball game, with the $300 still "burning a hole" in my pocket. It was then I made up my mind: I wanted to leave and get high, so I watched for the right moment. Predictably, we had another fight, and I packed up what little I had, and left.

I returned to live at my mother's house. By this time, she had divorced her second husband – the sodomizing, drug-addicted, fraudulent thief - and married a third husband. He was a decent sort who barely tolerated me and, not surprisingly, disapproved of my lifestyle of debauchery, drugging, and not going to church or family get-togethers. I'm surprised he allowed me in the house at all, and for good reason. Once there, I was back to my old tricks, and soon ended up across the river from St. Louis in East St. Louis, Illinois.

On the list of one of the poorest and most violent cities in the nation, East St. Louis is known for its poverty, crime, gritty industrial areas, strip joints, and hookers. Hookers with – I heard - access to the best crack. So, whenever I got paid, that's where I went to party and get high. The crack made me feel good, and having someone get it for me and join me in a seedy motel room provided attention and a high – both which I craved. The downside of the crack, of course, is that, once it was in my system, my sexual prowess plunged to zero. Zilch. This was pretty embarrassing, and didn't exactly elevate my feelings of manliness. I was ashamed, and felt guilty and worthless.

Somewhere inside of me, there was a stirring of conscience. I felt like a piece of trash for the things I'd done in my life, and at some level, reminded myself that I wanted to begin to climb out of the garbage dump I'd made of my life. But I kept going back with different girls a couple of times a week – same crummy motels, same dope, same embarrassing results.

Now, a healthy person… well, a healthy person wouldn't be in this mess… but let's say, a desperate person might wake up at this point and run for help. I was desperate, but obviously not desperate enough to run for help. So, with true addictive logic, I realized that, since it wasn't working so well for me in East St. Louis, I would change scenery, and run in a different direction: South St. Louis.

Einstein's classic definition of Insanity: "Doing the same thing over and over and expecting different results". Also repeated in Narcotics Anonymous.

There I was, age 45, back living in Mom's basement, and continuing to whine and blame everyone else for my problems. The scene in South St. Louis wasn't much different than it had been across the river. I was wasting $400-$500 a night on crack, more hookers, and motel rooms. I reasoned that I did it because of my upbringing or because no one really appreciated me. By continuing to delude myself that I was a victim of my past, my circumstances, others, etc., I justified my staying stuck in my addiction and my "stinkin' thinkin'". Victims can excuse themselves from taking responsibility and accountability because they are too busy blaming the world. That was me.

I decided to try my luck back in East St. Louis, which only proved that the definition of "insanity" fit me perfectly. I was robbed a couple of times, but that didn't stop me. Oh no. One night, after being robbed, I drove the hour back to my mother's house, got more money, and returned to where I had just been robbed, so I could party.

As a dog returns to its vomit, so fools repeat their folly. Proverbs 26.11

I wondered that, if I died, would anyone miss me? If I was dead, I reasoned, there would be no more misery, no more pain, and no more battles raging in my head. My journey to self-destruction increased in speed, destroying everything in my path, including myself. I was a sad mess. There's a saying that God watches over fools and drunks, and I was a perfect example of the latter two. I realized that, looking back later, God was indeed with me, even throughout those destructive, wasted, delusional years. Somewhere, in the fog and confusion, I continued to pray, though, despite my doubts about God's willingness or ability to answer my prayers, And I continued to get angry when I saw others receive answer to prayers while I searched the heavens for a sign.

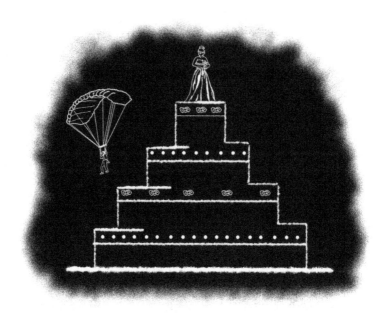

# Chapter Five: Marriage Ain't No Thing

## Nehemiah 8;10
*Do not grieve, for the joy of the Lord is your strength...*

I was living like a subterranean cellar-dweller in my mother's basement, working during the day at the lead processing smelter in Herculaneum, Missouri. As with the lead mines in nearby Bonne Terre where I moved as a child, the plant that processed the lead closed about the same time.

Once again, I found an old friend on Facebook whom I hadn't seen in over twenty years. I learned that Becky[8] had a crush on me when I was a skate guard at Spinning

8    Not her real name

Wheels. Our texting led to dating on the sly, because she was married. Becky said the marriage had been an unhappy one for a long time, which was justification enough for me (in my mind) to date her. It wasn't long before her husband moved out and they were divorced... and I was right behind him to ready to move in. She had a wonderful house on six acres in Desoto, as well as two beautiful children. Of course, I didn't consider how my presence in this relationship affected the children; all I knew was, life was good for me. Or so I thought.

To say that both of us came into the relationship with secrets and a tremendous amount of personal baggage would indeed be an understatement. We each brought trunk-loads of issues into the situation, not the least of which was my drug addiction. Trying to hide my addiction while feeding it at the same time was difficult, and became harder to maintain as time went on. Becky was bitter, angry, and upset that her marriage of twenty years had ended this way. Her self-esteem was at a low point, and I tried to build her up, but I certainly wasn't healthy enough to help her. I was still dealing with the same issues. I did love Becky, but now I look back and wonder if I loved her, or just wanted to be in love. Today I fully understand the difference, but then, perhaps I was just looking for another relationship in which I might experience love. Maybe I was just grateful to be out of my mom's house and have someone to take care of me, because I didn't know how to do it myself. Like all of my relationships, I looked for someone I thought could help me, fix me; someone who needed me. The reality of it is, of course, I couldn't help anyone because I didn't know how to help or fix myself. In fairness, I loved her the best way I knew how, but sadly, I realize how unfair it was her Becky and her children.

I continued to wear my many masks to cover my addiction, my insecurities, my sense of failures, not knowing who I truly was. Since my doctor was still giving me pain pills every month, I thought I was coping. It was coping through avoidance, at best. But it was a battle every second of the day, working, dealing with my mental turmoil, and being a boyfriend and a role model for her kids. I wore a happy face. I prayed and read the Bible every day, always asking God for help. Still, I continually lived with a feeling of discouragement in that area of my life, as well, thinking that even God wasn't there for me. Now I know that He was there for me the whole time, but I wasn't holding up my end; that is, my own relationship failures extended to my pursuing a relationship with God in the same way I pursued relationships with others: Superficially.

I was a hot mess, and then some. I couldn't see the light at the end of that long, dark tunnel. One moment I believed I was getting better, but my actions and thinking didn't reflect that. It was like being completely sucked into quicksand; as I thought I was pulling free, I would get sucked right back down into it, taking so many people with me.

In 2012, the smelter in Doe Run announced it would be closing December 31 of 2013. Of course, the wise plan would have been to begin looking for another job at that point; but you may have concluded that I was still much a stranger to wise planning. So, like everything else in my life, I stayed in the job until the end, hoping something would come along and bail me out. Sure, I told my girlfriend and everyone else that I was looking for a job, but I wasn't. I thought I needed to ride it out until the end, no matter the outcome, or whether I was happy or not. For another brief period of time, I had a false sense of security. But I'm getting ahead of myself; let me back up.

Before the plant shut down, a friend of mine introduced me to ICE. Yes! Jackpot! (For those readers who might be unfamiliar with the slang term, ICE is a highly-purified, crystallized form of Meth[9].) The crack and pain pills were not enough, as my addiction progressed into seeking out

9    Methamphetamine

more – or stronger – drugs to provide the same levels of high – or more – than I had during my years of illicit drug-using. I had used drugs for many years, but never shot up; I had just smoked. ICE was a new, exhilarating experience; a beast like nothing I had ever done. My libido went through the roof!

True to my addictive pattern of thinking and behavior, I was constantly trying to come up with reasons to leave the house and go get high. Even when Becky and I would go to a bar to hear a band, or with friends to a concert, I would be angry because I couldn't be high or drunk; always trying to hide the fact that my cravings were increasingly dominating my life.

That increased my irritability, as I continued to try to hide what I was secretly doing. Though Becky and I were an extremely intimate and active couple, I found myself watching porn every change I had. The relationship had its share of problems, but I wanted to continue it, for all of the wrong reasons, I think.

It was tough to finally begin looking for a job, hide my addictions, and pay attention to Becky. I tried to be who I thought I needed to be for the moment. I wanted to appear happy, even though it was becoming clearer that I wasn't. I didn't think I deserved happiness.

For those readers who have been or currently are going down this same dead-end road, you are not surprised that as my secret drug use continued, stealing became an inevitable part of the journey. I started stealing money from Becky, and when she confronted me, I denied it, just as I denied the severity of my addiction. I began to pawn things that were precious to her, and had some sentimental or financial worth; wedding rings, jewelry – anything of value. At the same time, I was doing the same thing to my mom. It was one of the worst feelings in the world to know exactly what I was doing to those who cared for me, and making an attempt to stop, but failing. Becky knew I had gotten high in the past, but was under the impression I had stopped. The fact that I could keep my drug usage from her reflects the depth of deception that many of us followed/follow in our addictions. Eventually we trip ourselves – and others – up, as our cravings and usage become so out of hand that we no longer care about the cost or who it hurts. For example, it was around this time that I stole some silver coins from my mom, and sold them for about fifty cents each. Afterwards, I discovered that they were each worth $180! I was so far gone by that time that getting my fix at the expense of others, disregarding all else, was my focus.

I continued to spiral downward; my sense of self-worth

and self-respect at an all-time low. What little faith I had mustered for God in the past was equally non-existent. Needless to say, my likability quotient had also hit rock-bottom, too, as I continued to lie, cheat, and steal my way deeper into my addiction. I clearly didn't like myself, and I decided that God didn't like me, either. Addiction is a self-centered disease, and among other delusions, addicts tend to see the world as revolving around ourselves. We imagine that people – and even God – need to meet us on our terms – even when we don't know what those terms are. "I want what I want when and how I want it" is an all-to-common mantra among those demonized by addictions of all kinds. Meeting and living "life on life's terms" was still a foreign concept. Meeting God on God's terms was something even more foreign.

I clearly didn't get it.

During my quest for an understanding and relationship with God, I had some tattoos of crosses on my shoulder and back, and began to imagine that God must be punishing me for having His cross on my body. I had shut Him out of my life, since the "sign" that He was with me had never visibly materialized. So, it is no surprise that I came to believe that God had abandoned me. God had left me to survive on my own. Oh, the thoughts that swirled in my head! I wanted the taunting thoughts that God had abandoned me to stop. I wanted to numb all the pain life had handed me – through the actions of others, and through my own actions. One night, I had a dream in which I saw a large, bright flash of light, and heard a voice speaking to me, though I couldn't hear what was said. I woke up in a sweat, freaked out, but didn't tell anyone about the dream. I was already questioning my sanity, so how could I admit to anyone that I was hearing the voice of God in my sleep? However, the door that I tried to close of that idea still remained open a crack. I now believe that God was trying to get my attention and talk to me, but I had shut him out, convinced that He could not possibly be interested in the life of a troubled addict like me. It took me a while to come to the realization that Jesus came to seek and save the lost. That was me.

Then in early 2015, my girlfriend kicked me out. She had plenty of reasons to do so. At that point, I felt completely hopeless.

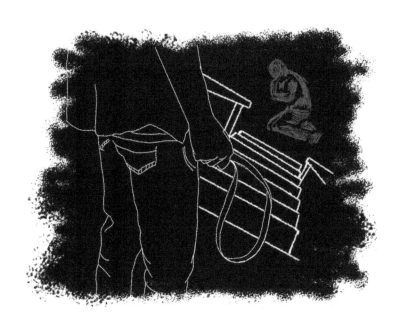

## Chapter Six: Why is God Punishing ME

**Luke 19:10**

*For the Son of the man is come to seek and to save that which was lost...*

Once again, I returned to my mom's house. If the reader gets a mental picture of the stereotypical loser returning to live in his mother's basement despite already growing up, you would get a picture of me at that point. Smoking dope, wallowing in self-pity and defending myself on all the reasons why Becky finally had the good sense to throw me out. Addicts are excellent manipulators, and I was good at it. I had years of practice in deceiving and lying to people, to convince others that

I wasn't using, that I had never stolen from the people closest to me. The fact is, I was a liar – lying to others, justifying my lying to myself. I was more concerned about my friends who were using than I was about the people who truly loved me. My family couldn't understand me. Not being inside my head, they had no idea what an addict thinks and feels. My not explaining it to them left no change that they would even try to understand me.

After the breakup, using ICE and craving sex intensified. I spent my time on porn sites, finding new friends to get high with, using hookers, visiting sex shops and truck stops, or going into a store, asking a female how they were doing, and hoping to get the response I was after. I was a predator who needed to feel wanted, desired, and appreciated. I had so many drugs in my system, I couldn't do anything but be embarrassed and ashamed.

I need to backtrack again.

Before my girlfriend kicked me out, I had bought a 2013 Chevy Malibu, which wasn't a great decision for me at the time; but then, my life seemed to be one long line of bad decisions after another. I got a part-time job delivering phone books in Desoto, and while I was doing that, I met a couple who needed a ride to Festus, so I obliged them. They introduced me to people who would add to my misery. A long-time friend had given me this job just to help me out. I worked all day, and continued to party all night, which continued to take a toll on me, as it would anyone. It wasn't long before I was back living with my mother, where I stole her debit cared to use on porn dating sites. I was still thinking that someone would want to hook up, and appreciate, accept, and love me. Boy was I wrong...again! Albert Einstein is said to have given the often-quoted definition of Insanity: "Insanity is doing the same thing, over and over again, but expecting different results." Those of us were/are active in our addiction and self-deception didn't/don't realize this truth until we begin our journey of recovery.

But I still didn't get that truth. Not yet.

Anyway, after a night of heavy partying, higher than a kite, I loaned my Chevy Malibu to someone so she could help her mother. I had a bad feeling about loaning her my car, and after work, I saw that my car still hadn't been returned. I found out shortly thereafter that the young woman who had done some heroin, got drunk, and wrecked my car! What else could go wrong? Why was God punishing me? What was all this happening? Why had my life been so difficult from the beginning? I had always tried to be nice to everyone, and didn't think I deserved having life hit me like that.

It's been said that life is 10% what happens to you, and 90% of what you do with it. To the out-of-control addict and others, life is viewed from the position of a victim; that is, minimize or deny the ways in which we dupe and control others, and play the role of the victim. The problem with this, of course, is that it's not only wrong, but it puts the blame on others – and on God – and excuses us from taking any responsibility for our actions and the decisions we make in life.

It got worse. Mom sat me down to talk about her debit card. I denied it, and was told to "get the hell out of the house". After all my mom had done for me – stuck up for me, enabled me, and loved me unconditionally – I had finally pushed her too far. She was the one personal who had always been in my corner, and I had treated her like this. I had stolen and pawned everything I could. When it came to me getting my fix, I treated her like everyone else. She was just a means to an end. Nothing else mattered at the time.

Three days after she told me to get out, she had to put my stepdad in a nursing home. She was on her way to visit him, and had a brain-stem stroke. I got the call from my sister, who told me the news. I was heartbroken. What did I do? I demanded God to tell me why He allowed this to happen to my mom... and right then, I hated God for every bad thing that had ever happened to me. First my car, now my mom. Rock bottom was getting closer.

For some reason, my ex let me stay with her after my mom's stroke. She later regretted it, because I hadn't changed. My mom was hospitalized; paralyzed on one side and not improving at all. My depths of despair were deep. I blamed myself for Mom's stroke, and was powerless to change her circumstances. I couldn't go visit her unless I was high. I'd sit in the car hitting a meth pipe so I could go inside and see her. I started praying, asking God to restore my mom. I wanted to atone for all my wrongs towards her. I wanted to hug her. I wanted my mom! We often hurt the ones we love and take them for granted, thinking they will always be there. This is especially true for those wrapped in the deception of addiction.

As Mom wasn't improving and I wasn't responsible, it was up to my sister to make decisions for her. One night at the hospital, with family around, I announced I was going to leave the hospital room and get something to eat. The money I had was burning a hole in my pocket. I did leave, but not for food: I found a hooker and got high. Crazy! I was feeling sorry for myself about Mom's stroke, my wrecked car, and not having a place to live. Down-and-out doesn't adequately describe my mental and physical state.

Without anywhere else to go, I began staying with people on some property in Hematite, MO; fifteen acres in the country, with a lot of dope. It was at this time that I began shooting, and the needle became my best friend. Sleeping in a garage built for working on cars was my new home. I had never been an extrovert or fit in easily, but now I didn't care. I was with people just like myself. We all imagined wanting and having the finer things of life, but at the end of the day, we swapped our dreams for getting high over anything else.

Days of not eating or showering were becoming more frequent. One night, I put whiskey in a spoon to break up the ICE in it, and stuck the needle in my arm. Two hours later, I was asked to drive a 49cc motor scooter from Barnhart back to Hematite, a distance of about 16 miles. I was jacked up on ICE and nervous about driving it, but I hopped on and drove off. At about midnight, that June 15, 2016, around a mile from the house, I swerved the scooter. My right leg slipped off the scooter, and I bounced on the road. Later I told everyone a deer had run out in front of me. I made it to the driveway which was long and rocky, got twenty feet up it and laid the scooter on its side.

For six long hours the pain was indescribable! I looked at my leg which was flat! I mean really flat! Scenes were flashing before my eyes; the traumas of my youth, the mental as well as sexual abuse - the years of addiction, and all the lives I had damaged, mine included. I screamed out in pain and prayed for God's help, praying that someone would find me out here. Again, I asked God, WHY? It wasn't until later, in my recovery, that He answered all my questions.

I tried to crawl up the driveway but it made the pain worse. It was the middle of the night, and I was sure I heard voices in the woods. I screamed for help that wasn't arriving. My leg looked as flat as an ironing board. Early in the morning I remembered that I had weed in my pocket so I threw it as far away from me as I could. Finally, someone on their way to work saw me and stopped. Thank goodness, help had come!

As I was put onto the stretcher and lifted up, it felt as though the bottom of my leg was sucked right to the top. I screamed out from the worst pain of my life and then passed out. I woke up later to see what I call a 'halo' holding my leg together. My ex was there, along with the state police who wanted to talk to me. The next day I was transported to Mercy Hospital in St. Louis. My sister showed up, and she unleashed all the anger, hurt and sadness she felt. I had let her down. I had betrayed and taken advantage of our mother. I became the family disappointment. I think her rage at me was largely due to her stress in dealing with our mom's stroke, but my actions had added to her emotional outburst. She let me have it to the point that she was asked to leave the hospital. I was heavily medicated, but still heard – and felt – every word she said. It made me feel like trash, again.

Over the next six weeks, I had eight surgeries and then rehabilitation. My girlfriend and her kids came to see me and she let me move in with them until I could walk again. She showed me great compassion, and I'm grateful to her for that. During that long hospital stay, I knew Mom had been moved to hospice care and wouldn't last long. When I received the call that she had passed, I became a basket case, and needed meds. to calm down. She was the one person who was always there for me and I felt responsible for her death. Once I was out of the hospital, I took bottles of pills many times, hoping to die, and then got angry because I didn't die and didn't have the guts to do it the right way. There was something deep inside restraining me; a sense that life would somehow be worth living, somewhere, somehow.

Eventually, the surgeries and rehab were over. I then had 90 days in a wheelchair, two months with a walker, and then on to crutches. It was hell. My girlfriend and I had issues again, which were my fault. So, I went back to the property at Hematite. These were "real friends "[10] who understood me, didn't judge, and realized I was just a good person caught in addiction. Or so I thought. I had a routine of making a monthly trip to Mercy Hospital in Festus, claiming I wanted to die. I had been doing this since Mom had the stroke and died. I thought if I could stay away from dope for a few days, when I got out of the hospital, I'd be strong enough to stay away from dope and friends who used. Addicts tend to think that way.

All the good intentions didn't help; that lasted about thirty seconds before I was back at it. Being at Hematite was constant, crazy nonstop partying again. I always thought the cops were watching us, but I didn't care. Since I wouldn't go into a store to steal or rob anyone, my job was to be the cleaning 'bitch'. Sometimes it felt degrading, but I had dope, so I was good. There was a dealer that kept breaking her teeth and didn't have a way to get them fixed. She asked for my dentures one night while we were high, and began cutting my dentures into individual teeth with needle nose pliers. After that, when she broke one of her teeth, she pulled one of mine out of a zip lock baggie, put glue on it and stuck it in her mouth.

---

10    In recovery parlance, we know these people to be "frienemies"; friends in addiction, but enemies to one's recovery.

Who the hell does that??

I was happy, I had dope. But in October of 2016, I couldn't stay on the property any longer. I had been voicing my opinion, which wasn't popular. One person, twisted and sick in her thoughts, accused me and others of touching her in a not so appropriate way. I was hurt. I had done many things in my addiction that were hurtful, but I had not touched anyone against their will, and everyone on the property knew it was a lie. It was time to move on. Now I look back on that situation, knowing it was a God-thing that it happened the way it did. A friend had bought me some dope with the agreement that I snort it. This was to be my last time doing dope out on the property, so he made it a good one. He put it on a stand-up mirror about three feet long. I snorted the dope feeling like a complete failure.

My time at the Hematite property was over.

## Chapter Seven: The Demons

**Psalm 34;18**
*The LORD is close to the brokenhearted and saves those*
*who are crushed in spirit...*

Once again, I needed a place to stay, and thought
of a lady I'd known and had kept in touch with over the
years. I knew she was living with her daughter and a girlfriend, and they agreed to let me join them. I was grateful
for a place with a roof, a shower, and occasional food.
There was a major problem with this arrangement, however: Needles and ICE were readily available, so shooting was the norm every morning and night. I liked being
there, but my presence was causing them problems. I

made plans, and left not long after Thanksgiving.

Back in the hospital I went. This time, when I was to be released, I had no home, no family, and no friends. I had nothing left. All the years of putting my addiction before all else; of lying, cheating and stealing to get what I wanted, had not served me well. I wanted to be a good person, but my thought processes and actions were clouded by drugs and alcohol. I ended up being dropped off in front of Larry Rice's homeless shelter in the City of St. Louis. I was forty-six years old, beaten down, broken, defeated, and scared. I stayed there one night and left.

For some time, I was wandering the streets scared and humiliated, hoping I wouldn't see anyone I knew. Despite all of my reckless living, I had never found myself without a place to live, and being homeless on the streets of St. Louis in the winter was an experience that will forever be etched in my memory – and not in a pleasant way. During the day, the homeless wait in the parks, behind buildings, next to the City Hall, shuffling around to stay warm; at night, they find their ways to shelters, if space is available. The weather was so cold, and I was fortunate to be able to stay at the Biddle House for a couple of days. Out on the street again, I met a guy who took me under his wing and taught me some pointers for survival on the street. Thank goodness for the St. Patrick Center, as well, for supplying me with essentials I needed to survive the bitter cold. If anyone had told me twenty or thirty years ago my life would end up like this, I would have laughed at them. All that I went through; I don't wish on anyone.

Living on the mean streets of the city was extremely dangerous. One night, someone high on K-2[11] nearly killed the guy I was hanging out with over something as ridiculous as cardboard! Are you kidding me? On the streets, everything that can help feed, protect, or warm someone can be coveted, and result in violence. I stopped the fight, called 911, and that night, figured it was time for me to get out of town. I got directions to the bus station from a police officer, and headed there. I was tired, hungry and scared, and desperately trying to come up with a plan. I asked the bus driver if I could ride for just a buck. Thank God he said yes!! On my way to South County, hoping to stay with people I remembered, I was also hoping for a shower, food, and warmth, but most importantly, dope. How crazy is that? I started the forty-five-minute bus ride, plus two miles after the bus trip, wanting drugs to numb the pain that was my life. Even worse, I wasn't sure the people I stayed with before would let me stay again. I had burned about every bridge I had crossed.

---

11     Synthetic cannabinoid, with the same active chemical (THC) as marijuana. Sometimes called synthetic marijuana.

Around midnight I arrived at their house. When they saw me in that condition, they must have had pity on me. I could stay, they said, even if only temporarily. For a couple of weeks, I had a routine. I would shoot ICE two or three times a day, clean house, and do anything else I could to help. I couldn't sleep. I was starting to get delirious and it was freaking them out. I couldn't blame them. Not eating or sleeping, I was just fighting the ever-present demons in my head taunting me that God hated me. I missed my mom. I just wanted to die.

With no definite plans, I left Butler Hill in early December at 4:30 in the morning, and walked in the freezing cold toward Arnold, MO. I had holes in my shoes the size of baseballs, but couldn't afford better. I was hoping to meet up with a girl from the past in hopes I could stay with her. I waited; she wasn't there. Walking all that way for nothing was disappointing. I stayed in Walmart for hours to get warm, but also to flirt with females hoping to get some positive attention. I wanted to feel wanted, by anyone. After frightening customers, mainly by how I looked and just by the way I was talking to them, I started the long walk back to Butler Hill. By this time, I had been up for at least thirteen days, could hear voices, and thought I was being followed. What was happening to me? Why was God punishing me? Why couldn't I talk to my mom?

Why, at age forty-six, was my life like this? I had always thought I was a good person; I tried to treat people the best I could or knew how. I had three failed marriages, many more failed relationships, and I had done great damage to others in my quest for affection and drugs. I had effectively destroyed my life and everything in it, including myself. The last time I saw my son was 1997. I still think of him every day.

All this was swirling in my head as I walked back to the apartment where I had been allowed to stay temporarily. I tried to figure out how to end it all. If I was dead, I would not be missed. I wouldn't be living this hell anymore. I had tried suicide before and it hadn't worked, but I'd never had the guts to do it the right way so it would work. Back at the apartment, I soon argued with my friends and was told to leave. This was a low for me, possibly the lowest point of my life. No longer welcome there, I started walking again toward Arnold, not sure of what I was doing or where I was going. Paranoia was setting in, the result of drugs, no sleep or food; I was sure people were following me to hurt me badly. If I saw someone with tattoos who was wearing a flat-billed cap, it meant this person was from my past and coming to get me. I could hear voices; everyone was guilty and I was going crazy!

I kept crossing back and forth across Highway 61/67 like

a ping pong ball with no destination in mind. The voices I heard kept asking, Why me? Why me? I was approaching the business district of Arnold, trying to stay focused on the people following me. I just knew if I stopped, I would be dead or badly hurt. I considered stopping so I could be killed or at least injured and then be in a hospital receiving pain meds., a bed, meals, and rest. I was a mental, physical and emotional mess. I kept going, bouncing from restroom to restroom to hotel, making sure I avoided the people who were relentlessly after me. I was tortured by the voices in my head, and prayed they would stop or I would die. I didn't care which, but please God, make it one or the other.

I walked into Gordmans, and within a minute collapsed onto the floor. Police and paramedics arrived, and I begged them to let me die. They, of course, told me they couldn't do that, but I pleaded with them to just turn away and go about their business. Thank God they didn't listen to me.

I was taken to the Hyland Center in South County, MO. The first four days there were a blur. I slept, awoke a few moments here and there to eat or see the doctor. After those initial four days, I was able to move around and visit my Case Manager. She asked me what I wanted. I responded that I was done; any fight left in me was gone.

I had rested, which allowed the voices to stop. My mind replayed the numerous mistakes I'd made and the trauma I suffered. I thought about the abuse I endured, how I had hurt my family, not feeling accepted, the chaos of years of addiction, wrecking cars when I was drunk, being held at gunpoint, being robbed and still going back. That was my life. It flashed in my mind like a fast-forward film.

The Case Manager knew I needed intensive therapy, and worked on finding a suitable placement for my needs. I had no health insurance, so I wasn't very hopeful. The places available were Bridgeway in St. Charles and SEMO in Farmington. Bridgeway had 1,000 people on a waiting list, but with me being an IV drug user, I was able to be admitted on Dec. 26th. The Hyland Center even covered the cost of my transportation to St. Charles.

While my actual clean date is December 19, 2016. I actually started my journey in recovery at Bridgeway the day after Christmas that year.

## Chapter Eight: A Son Returns Home

### Luke 15:24

*My son was dead and is alive again; he was lost
and is found...*

I had been to treatment before, but this time, I was ready
to devote myself to recovery. The first twenty-six days
in residential treatment at Bridgeway were busy for me,
learning why I did what I had done, why I had abandonment issues, why I couldn't have successful relationships,
why I hated myself. The big questions! There were no
more friends I could call on; I had burned all of my bridg-
es through my actions. No one was left for me to turn to
for help. This was the true bottom. I had arrived there a

broken man weighing only 160 pounds. There was no one to come visit me or bring me smokes, or for me to tell about my progress in recovery. I can now say I'm grateful for that; it gave me a chance to work on myself with no distractions and to dig deeper for the answers I needed.

One night in the apartment I dropped to my knees. While crying like a baby, I held my hands in the air and asked God for help. I had cried out to Him before, but this time it was different: I knew I couldn't walk this journey without Him. This time, I knew that He heard me, and answered my cry for help. He hadn't been silent all this time, as I had thought; He was waiting for me to come before Him in absolute submission. That night, I traded my broken life for the life of the One whose own life was broken on the cross for me. In that moment, alone with Him, I committed my life to Jesus, my Lord and Savior; the One who forgave my sins and my past, and promised He would never leave me nor forsake me. Together, we began a journey of healing and recovery that never ceases to amaze me day after day.

You are probably familiar with the Parable of the Prodigal Son which Jesus taught his disciples. It bears a quick re-telling, though, for those of you who, like me, may also be prodigals, and need a little reminder of how even prodigals can be restored.

The story goes like this: A son asked his father for his portion of his inheritance, gathered together all of his possessions, and went away to a distant land. There, he proceeded to waste everything his father had given him with wild living. After he had blown his inheritance, there was a famine in the land, and the son found himself feeding pigs and scrounging for food in the pig pens just to eat and stay alive. If you know anything about ancient Jewish history, a pig pen is the last place a respectable person would find himself/herself.

But this boy was beyond respectable: Hungry, homeless, beat-down, he had lost it all, including all those "friends" who were along for the ride until the money ran out. Maybe you can relate? Yet he had enough sense to decide to return home, hoping that his father would take him on as a servant. Not even as a son. A servant.

Then a miracle happened. When the father saw him coming, he didn't lock the gate, send servants to chase the young man away. No! The Bible tells us that when the father saw the prodigal son coming down the road (no doubt scrawny, stinking, with holes in his sandals), the father ran to him! Not only that, they celebrated. He was lost, and now found. Everyone else gave up on him… but the father never did.

Friend, if you're the prodigal, like I was, then maybe you're ready to leave the pigpen and come to the Father. God the Father. He won't turn you away. No, in fact, if you use your imagination and look in the distance, you'll see Him running toward you with open arms, welcoming you back to sanity, and life. There's forgiveness, wholeness, and safety in the Father's arms. That's where restoration and healing begin.

Since that moment, this prodigal has never looked back or given up. As I write this, I'm forty-eight months clean! I've traveled to fifteen states, stood in the middle of Time Square, spoken to the Missouri Baptist College football team, and many church groups. My life, while it isn't struggle free, is amazing! In treatment I was told to get a sponsor, do 90 meetings in 90 days and get a home group. I did all of that and more. I did 130 meetings in 90 days, all without a car!

To back up a bit, while living in the sober living house, I was going to outpatient treatment three days each week, seeing a trauma counselor once a week and hitting meetings every day. The first six months of recovery was a daily struggle. I hated it and loved it at the same time. Dealing with the feelings and emotions I had numbed for so many years was difficult and often overwhelming. I now knew that all these feelings as well as the pain I had caused others had to be dealt with in order for my recovery to progress. I began going back to the treatment center and talking to other clients new to recovery. That was such a blessing for me. I still stay in touch with a few of them. Sad to say, some are not with us any longer. Missing my mom and son, wanting them to know I was clean and getting stronger each day was something I wanted to share with them so badly.

Those of us in recovery recognize that trials will come; terrible cravings, nightmares, temptations of all sorts. A commitment to recovery and sobriety doesn't erase years of bad living all at once. A few months into my recovery, I began having some horrific dreams about using, as well as night terrors, and became afraid to fall asleep. I'm eternally grateful to the people in my network who helped me then. My relationship with God was most important and it was growing stronger. Slowly, my confidence began to get stronger also. Working a twelve-step program and making steady progress made me realize it was time to get my life back, and be proud of who I'd become. I was proud of 'Scott', for who I was, not what others wanted me to be.

To backtrack a little: When I was two or three months clean, still at the sober living house, I was able to stay out two or three nights a week. I put my big boy pants on and stayed with a friend of mine from the past who was also clean. She drove about forty-five minutes out of her way to come get me! I was excited to be going somewhere. Don't get me wrong; I'll always be thankful for the Bridge-way Sober Living House, but I also wanted a break. I went to my friend's house on Wednesday for a job interview on Thursday. On Thursday, my friend was sick and couldn't take me back, plus my phone wasn't working. I was stressed over this. It was April and still chilly outside, but I started walking and praying for a solution. I needed to get back to St. Charles. I walked about three miles before I saw a gas station. I kept praying, asking God to find me transportation.

Right after the prayer, a white truck pulled into the station. I was inside asking the clerk a question to which she didn't know the answer. The guy from the white truck comes in, buys a soda and he has the answer. I thanked him and went out the door to continue walking. The white truck pulled up next to me and it was the same guy. We talked a bit and he gave me a ride. He had worked a twelve-hour shift and was still willing to go two hours out of his way to drop me off in St. Charles! Talk about getting an answer to my prayer! I was overjoyed knowing the Lord had heard me and supplied my need!

# Chapter Nine: A True Test

**Jude 20**

*But you, dear friend build yourselves up in your most Holy Faith and pray in the Holy Spirit...*

From that point on, I never questioned anything that happened in my life. This was my spiritual awakening I had longed for! I thought, OK God, you didn't let me die when I wanted to, so You must have a plan and a purpose for my life. I was well into my recovery and still grateful to have been in the men's house, but mentally I was ready to move out. I no longer needed the accountability of turning in meeting sheets every week. I think my attitude showed it, too. I felt I was further along than other house members. I don't mean I felt I was better than them by any means, but I had no ties with anyone. I was in complete survival mode in a sense, so I was all about recovery. I was still going to meetings and working steps, learning about who I was as a person and why I did all the things that led me to this place in my life. I wanted someone to say "Atta boy, Scott, good job Scott". I was looking for instant gratification for the work I was putting in. The phrase 'fake it till you make it,' was me at first.

I was still looking for a job. My sponsor owned his own business, and even though I was without a driver's license, he paid me to drive him around. Sometimes we'd find a gym and work out, which was good therapy for me. Luckily, there was a gym within walking distance of the men's house, so I now had an activity to replace my old addiction. Also, my sponsor knew someone looking for help hanging drywall who would pay cash. I needed to get caught up on my rent, so this would work out for me. I talked to him and let him know where I was in my recovery. The next morning, he picked me up and we drove to a town about forty-five minutes away. I was determined to learn all I could about hanging drywall because I needed this work. Over the course of the day, the owner and another guy were shooting heroin in front of me. I prayed hard, called my sponsor, and made it through the day. I never went back. I wasn't willing to jeopardize the recovery I had worked so hard to achieve. Plus, I was still a work in progress.

At the gym the next day, I was talking about what had happened with the job. I was immediately offered a job there. Even though it was certainly a come down from the pay I was used to, I was grateful. I had been taught that humility was part of recovery. My job was to keep the gym clean, and I did it very well. Several clients and I got to know each other pretty well while I worked there, some who were also in recovery and were helpful and support-ive of me. No one judged me. I was locked into my recov-ery, although I still had emotions all over the place and dreams of using, along with night terrors.

Thank goodness I was still in outpatient care at Bridge-way, and on monthly Vivitrol shots to help with cravings. I kept hearing people say "Living life on life's terms," and finally, I was starting to understand what it meant. I was without family during recovery, and missing my mom, son, sister and her family was an everyday thing. How-ever, I realized there wasn't a thing I could do about it at that time in my life. I needed to continue pushing forward in recovery, so I did.

About this time, life showed up harder than it already had, or maybe my mind was less foggy than it had been for years. I was laughing one minute, crying the next, and then angry, all within minutes of each other. Up until I started my recovery, my life had been like quicksand. I was in a sinkhole, and each time I tried to climb out, when I thought I'd reached the edge, I was back in the middle, being pulled further down in a battle I thought I couldn't win.

Another trial was coming my way. I learned that a good friend of mine, who had gone into recovery nearly at the same time I had, had overdosed and died. She left Bridgeway for a women's sober living house. She did well there, which earned her a pass. While she was out of the house on the pass, she decided to get high one last time. She overdosed and was gone. I was heartbroken; this was the first time I had dealt with death while I was clean, and it was a true test for me. But with the help of my meetings, my new friends, and most importantly, my faith in God, I made it through this tough situation. Life was kind of crazy, but in a good way. I was working, and I was feeling emotions I had never felt before without drugs in my system. I met an amazing man on Facebook who became my life coach. It was for a brief time, but he played a huge part in changing my mindset on some things, and I'll always be grateful to him for his guidance. I began working at an Italian restaurant which was next to a gym, so, working two jobs and hitting meetings any chance I could, I continued building my foundation. Life was getting good! Being able to embrace my feelings and deal with them was an amazing feeling. I started to realize it was okay to have a bad day as long as I dealt with it in a positive way.

# Chapter Ten: A Vessel

## Psalm 16;11

*'You make known to me the path of life: in the presence there is*
*fullness of joy: at your right hand are pleasures forevermore..*

As I was enjoying life and finding Scott for the first time,
another Facebook friend reached out to me, asking for
advice about her daughter. After talking for a bit, she
guided me on my next journey in life. She became my
life coach, and was amazing at providing the toughness
and support I needed. She's another person I'll be forever
grateful to have known. We started hanging out quite a
bit and for the first time ever, I developed true feelings for
someone but kept them to myself. I felt I had nothing to

offer her; no car, no house, or much money, and most importantly, it was early in my recovery. When we no longer talked so frequently, I was crushed, but just kept working on me.

About this time, I moved out of the men's house to live with a friend I had met in rehab. Life was starting to really show up. I either walked or rode a ten-speed bike to work, which was close to ten miles each way. This was particularly grueling during the brutal St. Louis summers; transportation wasn't easy! I remembered back to when I would have walked any distance for dope, so I could do it now to be a productive member of society.

One day, riding the bike home from work, I was hit by a car! In that moment, I remember looking at the vehicle and thinking - there's no way this guy will pull out. Well, he did. The last thing I knew I flew over the hood of the car and then briefly blacked out. An ambulance took me to the hospital. I had bruised every rib on my left side and sprained my right wrist. Only when I was in tears at the hospital did I ask for something for pain. When I left the hospital, I didn't leave with a prescription, not wanting to tempt myself. For the next few months, I dealt with the pain as I worked and lived my life. If I had been in my addiction, the wreck wouldn't have stopped me from living my daily routine, so I didn't want it to stop my daily life as someone who was clean.

That summer, I walked to and from work in the 100-degree heat and lost a lot of weight. For the first time since beginning my recovery, I faced judgment from others. Some people I lived with began telling others that I must be using meth since I was losing so much weight. They didn't realize I was walking and working in extreme heat every day. This made me angry, and thoroughly upset. I called my sponsor. Thankfully, he opened my eyes to how people are. People judge not to tell you how they feel about you; they judge based on what they see in themselves. That is true! A couple of weeks later, those two guys were kicked out of sober living for failing drug tests.

At nine months into recovery, I had the opportunity to speak to the Missouri Baptist University football team about God, and how we are all one decision away from changing our lives for good or bad. I was humbled and honored to speak with these young men. As life kept getting better and my passion for people got stronger, I learned more about myself and others. I had made great strides in my life, but I knew my decision-making still needed work. As recovery is a journey lived moment-by-moment, it takes time to unlearn and correct our using behaviors, and after 30 years in addiction, I had plenty of unlearning and relearning to do! I still wanted what I wanted when I wanted it - right now! I made decisions without thinking them through or asking for advice. Often, it didn't end well, but it was a valuable learning process. I'm still working on this today.

My life was going well. My faith in God was growing stronger, and I was leaning on Him more and more, and giving Him all the glory. I worked two jobs and loved life. Even on the bad days, I would not give up because I always wanted to do well and learn more about myself. I was busy on Facebook, sharing a lot about God, recovery, and life in general. Among other things, I was given an opportunity to be interviewed by a friend I'd met online that was doing a series on addiction in Cincinnati, Ohio. I was honored he'd chosen to interview me. I was building a network of amazing new people, my faith in God was growing stronger, and my dreams of using were not happening as often. I was still working on keeping thoughts of the past at bay. Sometimes I'd be happy, when out of the blue, thoughts of using or killing myself would overwhelm me. All I could do was pray to God for strength, guidance and wisdom, and reach out to my network of great people, hit a meeting, or go to church. I stayed clear of relationships, even though a few women had my attention. I still felt I had nothing to offer at this point. During active addiction, I would have brought people into my chaos, and I didn't want to do that again. Until I had full confidence in myself, I didn't want to bring anyone into my life.

Around this time, a woman from Las Vegas reached out to me, asking advice on what to do about her husband. We became friends. This situation was starting to happen more often, and I saw God's true purpose for me; His plan from the beginning, His way of using me as a vessel once I fully surrendered to Him became clear to me. As I realized this, I was overcome by a rush of tears thinking that God would want to use someone like me! I continued reading the Bible and developed a better understanding of how God works.

When I was thirteen months clean, this same friend asked if I would be interested in speaking at some treatment centers in Las Vegas. I was thrilled to be asked, but it never worked out. We continued to talk and stay in touch. Feelings developed and we tried a long-distance relationship, and I even spent a week in Las Vegas with her. I didn't have the time to devote to her that she deserved, and we ended the relationship. She was an amazing woman; that's how I remember the time with her, and we're still good friends.

## Chapter Eleven: There For A Reason

### Psalm 20;4-5

*May he grant you your heart"s desire and fulfill all your plans! May we shout for joy over your salvation, and in the name of our God set up our banners! May the Lord fulfill all your petitions!'*

This was a time of substantial growth for me. I hadn't been to Las Vegas in eighteen years. My last trip involved staying at the Luxor, and I was so high I couldn't find my room. Returning to that city clean was like coming full circle for me. I walked into the hotel shaking, hoping my nerves wouldn't get me down. We were able to walk around, even gamble a little, but I had no desire to use, which was huge for me. Recovery and sobriety were allowing me to clear my head, and during the time I spent with the Lord, I realized He was pointing me in another direction: After years of lying and manipulating people, I began to realize that I had such a passion for people, and that the Lord was preparing me a new direction and a purpose that was far greater than myself and anything I could've imagined.

At last, I got it!

During those dark years, deep in my addiction and pain, I could never have imagined that the God I thought was so elusive was present with me the whole time. Until I was willing to cry out to Him in utter despair and surrender, I could only imagine that He had turned His back to me, a run-down, homeless addict. Nothing could be further from the truth!

During my early recovery, I began putting my story on Facebook. Originally, I was doing it just for myself, and never in my life did I expect it to explode the way it did! I'd write part of my story, and then say, "I get it". That caught on big time. As I continued to pray and ask God what He would have me do for Him, I got the idea of having T-shirts, hoodies, and hats made with the slogans Just for Today and I Get It printed on them. I thought that maybe I could give a portion of the proceeds to charities which helped families who had lost loved ones to addiction pay for funerals. After more research and talking with knowledgeable people, I realized it wasn't the time or the method. Maybe one day, God willing, the merchandise will take off, and I'll help people without resources get into sober living.

By this time, I'd had two life coaches, both of whom were fantastic, and each having a different approach to coaching. Working together with these trained individuals awakened in me a desire to learn more about people, and to learn more about people in order to begin traveling to carry a message of hope. Slowly, God was opening doors to allow me to do that.

Sarah, an online friend, and I had a chance to visit Pennsylvania for a recovery event, so I rented a car and away we went, making stops in West Virginia, Ohio, and Pittsburgh, before we reached Allentown. We attended a meeting with a man I have great respect for. All day Saturday was spent at a recovery event. On this inspiring trip, we drove about 3,000 miles in four days, and met people I will always remember.

With the trip over and back to my daily routine, I continued to stay clean. Some days were harder than others, but by pushing through the tough times, I could see personal growth in myself. I had lost many friends to overdoses, was not yet making the money I wanted, had no car, and was living with other people. These factors caused me to question my thoughts. Someone I had great respect for told me I was right where I needed to be. It was a bitter pill to swallow, but I grew to understand that he was right.

I continued to travel with trusted people as the Lord gave me opportunity. One such trip with a recovery friend took us to Time Square in New York City. Visiting the 911 Memorial was a sobering, somber event. Imagine, two drug addicts that had lived on the street and had nothing, we able to make this trip, and stand before this memorial to the thousands who had lost their lives in a senseless attack.

I was eager to hear my friend's life story, and learn how far she had progressed in her recovery and witness her growth. It was a special time for us both, celebrating our recovery, and seeing life again with new eyes. We were learning to experience the joy of even the smallest of life's events, including buying hot dogs from a vendor's cart on the streets of New York City. If you visit there, try them!

Near this time, I was getting a settlement from being hit

by a car the previous year, which allowed me to travel more. I had a trip planned with friends from social media, and our journey would take us over a few states. It's amazing how God works when we're praying for His guidance. I bought a 2016 Dodge Dart, thankful for the blessing of a car, and in mid-July, we took off!

I headed to Crossville, TN to finally start putting names with faces I knew from online. During this trip, I was driving through Illinois in the middle of the night, getting ready to celebrate nineteen months clean, so excited about life and the journey I was on. Out of nowhere, my mind flashed: "Hey, you're by yourself; you could stop at one of these many strip clubs, have a drink, and no one would know."

Wow! I started praying and calling people, using the tools I'd learned in treatment. Thankfully, I made it to my friend's house early the next morning. We headed to a state park north of Knoxville to pick up another guy. I was super excited. To think that not so long ago I was shooting dope and homeless, couch-surfing and living on the streets. Now, I'm traveling and bringing the hope I had so desperately sought – and found - to others in addiction who need it. Praise God! I have a message of hope and redemption to share!

During this trip, we were sitting at a picnic table, talking about God, recovery and life, and decided to go live on Facebook as part of a recovery group we participate in. We were alone; the visible trails through the park were empty – not a soul in sight. When my friend was nearly finished speaking and mentioned recovery, out of no-where this young man came walking up and said, "Did you guys say something about recovery?" The hair on our arms stood up! The young guy sat down and shared his story with us. He had recently moved to the area, had seven months of sobriety, but had messed up. He was upset, needing someone to talk to. Bam! We were there for him! God is working among us! I love it when His presence is felt! To this day, that young man is sober and doing well! It was an amazing day.

On July 20th, I had planned to drive to Cincinnati, OH to meet my buddy who had interviewed me when I was nine months sober. The next day we planned to go on to Bedford, TX, to meet another online friend. I was really looking forward to this meeting. We met up and I de-cided I'd follow him in my car since the trunk was full of Just For Today I Get It T-shirts. We were on the highway when the clutch in my car went out! I had bought it six days earlier and now this! I was sitting on the side of the highway at 4:30 P.M. on a Friday. I was disappointed, and asked God to show me the big picture of this situation. Once again, He showed me the very next day! I sat in that broken-down car for four hours, trying to call the dealership and warranty company, and getting nowhere but frustrated.

During my wait on the highway, I had my car searched. It was a new car with temporary tags and NA key tags on my key ring. This time I could smile, knowing there was nothing illegal to find. I'm clean! The State Troopers and I talked about recovery and how bad the opioid epidemic had become. They were cool. A tow truck driver finally picked me up and agreed to take me to a cheap hotel he knew about, but after talking with him about God and recovery, he knew he didn't want me to see the drugs and hookers which would be at this particular hotel. He took me to another one which cost more than I wanted to spend, but I did it, anyway.

You can't put a price on recovery, and God will put you just where He wants you for a particular reason. And if He orders it, He'll make sure the cost is covered.

The next morning at 7:30, I was outside having a smoke and coffee. I noticed a gentleman on a bench, looking upset. We began talking, and I learned he was in from Indiana, looking at a job. He had lost everything back home because of 35 years of drinking, and now he was looking to make a new start. Regardless of the job situation here, he had to return to Fort Wayne for a short time. He was on day seven of no drinking, and wanted a drink so badly he was shaking. Here he was, away from home, with no one he knew to talk to. I knew God had put me in this hotel to talk to this man. That's how God works! He had taken the fact that my car broke down to use me to help this stranger at the hotel.  When I think about this plan that God unfolded in front of me, and also the young man we spoke with at the state park in TN, I get chills!

Have you ever heard it said that there are no coincidences with God?  There's aren't.

God wasn't finished working through me during that particular trip. My original plan had been to leave our location Saturday morning and drive to Bedford, TX, to see a friend, but since my car was at the dealership at least through Monday, I decided to fly. I booked a flight online and a buddy took me to the airport.  I was thankful I was still able to visit with Jennifer. We'd had many conversations on the phone and through Messenger. I could see she was a strong woman completely vested in her recovery. She picked me up at the airport and let me crash on her couch that night. It was an awesome experience hanging out and getting to know someone, and talking about life with no expectations.

The next morning as I was crossing the street to get my energy drink and smokes, I was wearing one of my Just For Today I Get It shirts. Standing there was a man buying alcohol and laughing, and asked me the meaning behind my shirt. I quickly obliged. He asked me to put his number in my phone and call him, so he'd have my number. He added that he might need to call me sometime. Absolutely! Glad to do it.

Later that night, when Jennifer went to sleep, I was lying on her couch at complete peace. What a feeling! I reflected on the fact that twenty months ago I was a needle junkie, freezing my butt off, living on the streets of St. Louis with no hope, begging God to let me die. I contrasted that with my life today. Now I was clean and sober. I was traveling to different areas of the country to tell other addicts about God, recovery and life. What a wonderful transformation God had woven into my heart and soul!

I attended a meeting in Bedford while I was there. At the end of my visit with Jennifer, we were at a restaurant before we went on to the airport for my return to CVG in Kentucky. My phone rang. It was the guy I'd met who was buying alcohol! He wanted me to know he had attended his first AA meeting. My words of hope and recovery and my own personal story had inspired him! The phone call was to thank me. Praise God! I had tears rolling down my face, humbled that God used me to make a positive impact on this man. Jennifer and I had a wonderful time at dinner, and then it was time to leave.

## Chapter Twelve: This Is Not The End

### Joel 2:25

*I will restore the years that the swarming locust has eaten...*

I can't believe my life is this good now! All the pain I carried for so long, the destruction I caused others, thinking that God hated me, had forgotten me, and completely abandoned me, had healed. Today, I know that God was with me all the time. He was there, waiting on me to want Him. There were many times I should have died, but I'm still here today. Which brings me to this: as my faith grows stronger each day and I continue to grow emotionally as a person, my wish is for everyone to have peace in their hearts, joy in their smile, and compassion with themselves and their treatment of others.

This is not the end of my story. It is, in fact, part of a new beginning that could only be found through humbly submitting my brokenness to the God of Glory. He's the Father that ran down the road to meet me when I cried out to him that winter night as I began my recovery. We're walking together down a new road now... and you can walk down that same road with us.

You may not have any more to offer Him in exchange for your life than I did: Broken dreams, broken lives, a trail of disappointment, hurt, and failure. Like the kid in the pigpen. Please, don't stay in that place – begin the journey home.

It is said often that we don't begin our journey to recovery and restoration of sanity until we "hit bottom" – whatever or wherever that may be for each of us. For me, it began with my unknowingly living out the first three of the Twelve Steps: I recognized I was powerless and that my life was totally unmanageable; I believed that there was a power greater than myself who could restore me to sanity; and I made the decision to turn over my will and life to Him. In essence: I couldn't, I knew Somebody who could, and I made the decision to turn it all over to Him.

That simple? Well, that's the starting point. The transfor-mation doesn't happen overnight, you know. After years of destructive thinking and behaviors in our addictions, making radical life changes begins with the simple deci-sion to take the first step... and when you do, you'll rec-ognize that our Father God is right there, waiting to take your hand. Even running toward you.

If you're a parent, the analogy of a child taking its first steps as a baby will make sense. Those first steps are faltering, teetering, awkward. Babies may fall face-first – or bottom-first – to the floor, until they learn to stand and walk. Notice, they may fall down, but they get back up and keep trying. We may fall face-first at times, too. First steps are usually the toughest. But as a wise and loving parent, you were there, with arms outstretched, waiting to catch the toddler, holding his/her hands, and cheering those clumsy successes.

# A New Day & What Scott is Doing

Outside of writing this book I'm involved in outlets that keep me motivated and helping to stay sober. I do this for myself, but it has also given me the ability to help guide and save others who are ready to make a change.

Getting ordained, was a step I've taken to become closer with God and learn further about the journey he has for all of us. It was a way to allow my ministry to grow and find more about who I am and what God's purpose and mission for Scott is.

My Ministry, Vision of Redemption, is a place to lose the stigma of the church and be an outlet for those that have been where I had come from. No judgement, no stereotypes, but just simply as place to allow God to enter and grow in those people looking for something missing in them. Live each day just for today not for tomorrow. As it has not come and we cannot change yesterday!

Soon to come will be my online podcast / videocast allowing others to share their stories and give my ministry and others battling their own struggles a voice to share their journey and what tribulations they are overcoming.

In 2020 I became the recovery outreach director for First Assembly's Church Celebrate Recovery. My involement with my church family is being the voice in the community and assisting those with finding sobriety homes, detox facilities, and treatment centers.

## *To learn more or get help please use the links below:*

**Vision of Redemption - Ministry:**
*www.visionofredemption.com*

**Celebrarte Recovery:**
*www.firstassemblychurch.org/celebraterecovery*
*www.celebraterecovery.com*

**National Suicide Prevention Lifeline:**
*Available 24 hours*
*800-273-8255*
*www.suicidepreventionlifeline.org*

# A Special Thanks

To the many people that have helped me along my
journey and in writing this book.

**Photography:**
Glam To Glory Photography

**Editioral and Support:**
Rose Mary Sellards
Kate Mansfield, MA, MBA, MA
Richard Viehmann

**Support:**
Katie Fortuna, Recovery Pastor
Dale Mansfield, Threestand STL

*To God be The Glory*

# Words of Reflection

Any one that is in recovery from a substance use disorder or has a loved one enduring a substance abuse disorder get this book read this book!

As a person in long term recovery myself I understand how cunning and baffeling addiction can be not only to the person experiencing it but to those around them.

The author is vulnerable in sharing the depths his addiction took him a key to connecting with the still suffering addict. And then the transformation the struggles the author endured in addiction became the places God now uses him to connect with the still suffering addict. Let this book become a valuable tool to share not only the hope of recovery but to allow you to build a lense of empathy rather than judgement when you see a person Struggling with a substance abuse disorder.

Great job keeping the message simple yet powerful.

**Christine C McDonald**

*Author and National advocate for addiction, re entry and victims of sex trafficking*

# Scott Hartmann

It has been my pleasure to know Scott Hartman in a friendship that has gone from mere acquaintance to a partnership in ministry. I have watched him grow in his relationship with Christ Jesus to the place where his heart burns with the desire to go deeper and deeper to help those that are afflicted. I have appreciated and admired the contributions this man has brought to the homeless and the recovery community in St. Charles County and the St. Louis Metropolitan area. He continues to carry the hope and love of the Father to those who feel lost, broken and hopeless.

I have always loved reading autobiography's and this book is unfiltered and true to the heart of Scott, barring nothing but raw truth. Scott has had many vast experiences. Dirty, nasty and ugly experiences laced with God given gifts of freedom, grace and triumph will give his readers a truth they can relate to in their own lives.

The Bible says that those who are forgiven much, love much. Scott is a true life story of how love can find us in our broken places and turn the love we have received to penetrate the hardest heart and reach the lives around us.

This book will, without a doubt make a difference in the lives of those who read it. Scott has taken a long journey in his life and he has candidly opened that up to share his journey with the readers. His book

moves through an emotional spectrum of neglect, abuse and hatred in the long road home through grace, mercy, and love. This is truly a story of the power of God to take a life of hopelessness and show that no matter what has been done to us or what dark path we find ourselves on, there is a God who can turn it around to make all things new. God shows through Scott how he can take what the world sees as a broken hopeless drug addict to a man who earnestly spends his life committed to literally snatching others from deaths door with the hope, power and love that now dwells within him!

**Katie Fortuna**
Recovery Pastor FAC

# FROM CHASING DOPE TO PUSHING HOPE

**My Steps To Recovery & Redemption**

Scott Hartman

"Courage, determined, and survival are three words I would describe about this book.

Scott gives a raw experience into his drug and alcohol addicted life and through his journey in finding God.

No matter if you aren't an addict, this book can resonate with a lot of people. From the abusive father, not belonging, seeking approval, to the quest to find Him in your life, this book is a must read."

Lindsey Seals
Executive Mansger
Sober Living House

Made in the USA
Las Vegas, NV
25 June 2022